WIGGLESWORTH SMITH on FAITH

A 30-DAY DEVOTIONAL

W9-AWZ-908

Edited and Compiled by
Larry Keefauver

CREATION HOUSE

Creation House
Strang Communications Company
600 Rinehart Road
Lake Mary, FL 32746
Phone: 407-333-3132
Fax: 407-333-7100

All Scripture quotations are from
the King James Version of the Bible.

A word about the cover:
The writing in the background is the actual
handwritten letter that Smith Wigglesworth
started the day before he died. His letter
shares the details of the healing of a woman
from cancer through his ministry.

Introduction

elcome to this thirty-day journey of faith with Smith Wigglesworth, the humble, anointed servant of God who dramatically shaped the early Pentecostal and Holiness movements on the continent and in the States. What is so intriguing about this uneducated English plumber? As I began my research, I found myself mesmerized by the original sermon notes, Bible studies and pamphlets of Smith Wigglesworth. Delightful nuggets of spiritual truths filled those brown, aging pages from the past.

The purpose of this devotional series is to share some of the original Smith Wigglesworth with you. I pray that your relationship with the Lord, your walk in the Spirit and your intimacy with the Father will deepen as you read afresh the words God gave a humble plumber who brought revival to his generation.

We have kept our editing of Wigglesworth to a minimum. While his language may be unpolished at times, the force and power of his expression will speak to your life.

Called a "twentieth-century apostle," Wigglesworth became a legend as God used him in an evangelistic and healing ministry. Born in 1859 in Menston, Yorkshire, England, he was converted in a Wesleyan Methodist meeting at age eight and pursued a career in plumbing. He married Polly Featherstone, and he and Polly operated a little mission in Bradford, England.

In 1907, in Sunderland, the forty-seven-year-old Wigglesworth received the baptism of the Holy Spirit, which radically changed him and transformed his ministry into a worldwide phenomenon. Literally thousands were saved and untold scores were healed by God's power as Wigglesworth preached powerful messages throughout the world. He went home to the Lord he loved in 1947 at the age of eighty-seven.

This booklet brings to you some exquisite gems of revelation about faith. Wigglesworth would often challenge his listeners by saying, "Faith is an act. Faith is a leap. Faith jumps in. Faith claims. Faith's author is Jesus. He is the author and finisher of faith."

Each devotional contains a scripture, a principle about faith and a prayer. Receive power and inspiration for your daily walk with the Lord as you read the words of Smith Wigglesworth.

I give all honor and praise to God the Father and Jesus Christ the Son for sending the Holy Spirit to inspire servants like Smith Wigglesworth to share such glorious truth and revelation so that mine and future generations might be truly blessed in Him!

Larry Keefauver, editor
1996

EXCERPTED: Bible study no. 8, 15 July 1927, 13.

The Amen of Faith

*Now faith is the substance of
things hoped for, the evidence of
things not seen.*
Hebrews 11:1

I believe there is only one way to all the treasures of God and that is the way of faith. There is only one principle underlying all the attributes and all the beatitudes of the mighty ascension into the glories of Christ, and it is by faith. All God's promises are *Yea* and *Amen* to them that believe.

You get to know God by an open door of grace. He has made a way. It is a beautiful way that all His saints can enter in and find rest. The way is the way of faith. There isn't any other way.

God wants us with the Amen that never knows anything else than Amen — an inward Amen, a mighty moving Amen, a God-likeness Amen. That which says, "It is, because God has spoken. It cannot be otherwise. It is impossible to be otherwise."

Beloved, I see all the plan of life where God comes in and vindicates His power by making His presence felt. It is not by crying, nor groaning. It is because we believe. And yet, we have nothing to say about it. Sometimes it takes God a long time to bring us through the groaning and crying before we can believe.

Pray this closing prayer today:

Jesus, through the power of Your Holy Spirit, I seek the gift of supernatural faith that I may penetrate the heavenlies, seeing the things of God. Amen.

EXCERPTED: "Faith (Part Two)," message presented at Glad Tidings Tabernacle, 3 August 1922, 1.

Overcoming Faith

For whatsoever is born of God overcometh the world: and this is the victory that overcometh the world, even our faith.

1 John 5:4

To believe is to overcome. I am heir to all the promises because I believe. A great heritage. I overcome because I believe the truth, and the truth makes me free.

Christ is the root and source of our faith. When He is in what we believe for, it will come to pass. No wavering. This is the principle: He who believes is definite. A definite faith brings a definite experience and a definite utterance.

Faith Principle #2

There is no limit to the power

that God will cause to come upon those who cry to Him in faith. God is rich to all who will call upon Him.

Lay in your claim for your children, your families, your co-workers, that many sons may be brought to glory. As our prayers rest upon the simple principle of faith, nothing shall be impossible to you.

The root principle of all this divine overcoming faith in the human heart is Christ. When you are grafted deeply into Him, you may win millions of lives to the faith. Jesus is the Way, the Truth and the Life, the secret to every hard problem in your heart.

Pray this closing prayer today:

Lord Jesus, grant me overcoming faith to claim the impossible. Amen.

EXCERPTED: "Believe! The Way to Overcome," Faith Leaflet No. 1.

Believe That God Is Greater

*So then faith cometh by hearing,
and hearing by the word of God.*
Romans 10:17

Don't stumble at the Word. If Jesus says anything, if the Word conveys anything to your mind, don't stumble at the Word.

Faith Principle #3

Believe that God is greater than you are, greater than your heart, greater than your thoughts.

Only He can establish you in righteousness even when your thoughts and your knowledge are absolutely against it.

Often I find that people misunderstand God's Word. They bring their mind to the Word, and because the Word does not exactly fit their mind, they do not get liberty. They want the Word to come to their mind. It will never do it. You have to be submissive to God.

The Word of God is true. If you will understand the truth, you can always be on line to gain strength, overcome the world and make everything subject to you.

Pray this closing prayer today:

Lord Jesus, I confess that Thy Word is greater than my thoughts, my feelings, my opinions and my ways. Renew my mind according to Thy Word. Give me a desire for the kind of faith that will overcome my world. Amen.

EXCERPTED: "Sons of God," Bible study no. 7, 14 July 1927, 4.

Saved Through Faith

*For by grace are ye saved through
faith; and that not of yourselves:
it is the gift of God.*
                              Ephesians 2:8

human faith works and then waits for the
wages. That is not saving faith. Then there is
the gift of faith. "For by grace are ye saved
through faith; and that not of yourselves: it is
the gift of God." Faith is that which God gave
you to believe. "Whosoever believeth that
Jesus is the Christ is born of God" (1 John 5:1).

Faith Principle #4

***The sacrifice is complete, and
God has kept you because you
could not keep yourself.***

We read in 1 Corinthians 12:9, "To another

faith by the same Spirit." When my faith fails, then another faith lays hold of me. One time I thought I had the Holy Ghost. Now I know the Holy Ghost has got me.

There is a difference between our hanging onto God and God's lifting us up. There is a difference between my having a desire and God's desire filling my soul. There is a difference between natural compassion and the compassion of Jesus that never fails. Human faith fails but the faith of Jesus never fails.

Pray this closing prayer today:

Jesus, thank you for lifting me up. Thank you for filling my soul with an awareness of your great desire for me. I seek You for the faith that never fails. Amen.

EXCERPTED: "Overcoming," message presented at a Pentecostal camp meeting in Berkeley, Calif., 3 June 1924, 5.

Two Kinds of Faith

Wherefore also we pray always for you, that our God would count you worthy of this calling, and fulfil all the good pleasure of his goodness, and the work of faith with power.
2 Thessalonians 1:11

There are two kinds of faith that God wants us to see. There is a natural faith and there is a saving faith. All people are born with the natural faith. Natural faith has limitations. Saving faith is a supernatural gift of God.

There is the gift of faith. It is the faith of Jesus given to us as we press in and on with God. I want to put before you this difference between our faith and the faith of Jesus.

Faith Principle #5

Our faith comes to an end.

Most people have come to where they have said, "Lord, I can go no further. I have gone so far and I can go no further. I have used all the faith I have, and I just have to stop now and wait.

As I saw in the presence of God the limitation of my *natural* faith, there came another faith, a *supernatural* faith that could not be denied, a faith that took the promise of God, a faith that believed God's Word.

Pray this closing prayer today:

Holy Spirit, give me supernatural faith as I press in and on with God. As I confront the circumstances of my life daily, help me to exercise my faith with Your power. Amen.

Excerpted: "Faith (Part Two)," message presented at Glad Tidings Tabernacle, 3 August 1922, 3.

The Trial of Faith

*That the trial of your faith, being
much more precious than of gold
that perisheth, though it be tried with
fire, might be found unto praise
and honour and glory at the
appearing of Jesus Christ.*
1 Peter 1:7

Gold perisheth. Faith never perisheth. It is more precious than gold, though it be tried by fire. I went to a place one day and a gentleman said to me, "Would you like to see purification of gold this morning?"

I replied, "Yes."

He got some gold and put it in a crucible and put a blast of heat on it. First it became blood red, and then it changed and changed. Then this man took an instrument, passed it over the gold which drew off a substance that was foreign to the gold. He did this several times until every part was taken away. Then at last he put it over again and said, "Look." There we both saw our faces in the gold. It was wonderful.

The trial of your faith is much more precious than gold which perisheth.

Faith Principle #6

When God so purifies you through trials, misunderstandings, persecution, suffering and being wrongfully judged, Jesus has given you the key; rejoice in that day!

Beloved, as you are tested in the fire, the Master is cleaning away all that cannot bring out His image, cleaning away all the dross from your life, all the evil, until He sees His face reflected in your life.

Pray this closing prayer today:

Lord, I rejoice in my trials and sufferings as You refine my faith so that my life may reflect You. Amen.

EXCERPTED: "Rising Into the Heavenlies," address presented in Wellington, New Zealand, 24 January 1924, 8-9.

Living Faith
Makes Us New

*Therefore if any man be in Christ,
he is a new creature: old things
are passed away; behold, all things
are become new.*
2 Corinthians 5:17

Now my heart cries out for a living faith with a deep vision of God. The world cannot produce it. Living faith is a place where we seek the Word so that when we pray we know God hears. Living faith comes into the presence of God, asking Him and believing Him for the answer, while having no fear.

I used to have a tremendous temper, going white with passion. My whole nature was not what God wanted. God knew that I could never be of service unless I was sanctified. For example, I was difficult to please at the table. My wife was a good cook, but there was always something wrong. After God sanctified me, she testified in a meeting that from the time God touched me, I was pleased with everything she cooked.

It is our human spirit that has to be controlled by the Holy Spirit.

Faith Principle #7

There is a place of death to self where Christ reigns in the body. Then all is well.

This word is full of stimulation. It is by faith, into a place of grace that all may see us new. Behold! Behold! Behold! What is it? The Holy Ghost is arousing our attention. He has something special to say. Behold, if you will believe, you can be sons of God in likeness, character, spirit and actions.

Pray this closing prayer today:

Lord Jesus, I desire to be changed in Thy Presence. Make of me a new creation in Thee. Amen.

EXCERPTED: "Now! Now! Now!," message presented in Colombier, Switzerland, n.d., 2-3.

Only
Believe

*As soon as Jesus heard the word
that was spoken, he saith unto the
ruler of the synagogue, Be not
afraid, only believe.*

Mark 5:36

Only believe, only believe.
All things are possible,
Only believe.
Only believe, only believe.
All things are possible,
Only believe.

The importance of that chorus is the word *only* right in the midst of the chorus. If I can get you to see that when you get rid of yourself, all human help and everything else, and *only* have God behind you, you have reached a place of great reinforcement and continual success.

If you help yourself, to the measure you help yourself, you will find there are limitations to the life and power of God in you.

Faith Principle #8

I find so many people trying to help themselves. What God wants is an absolute, entire clinging to Him.

The one grand plan God has for us is *only believe*.

Absolute rest. Perfect submission. God has taken charge of the situation. You are absolutely brought into everything God has, because you dare only believe what He says.

God would have me press into your heart a living truth — only believe!

Pray this closing prayer today:

Jesus, what You have said I believe. Amen.

EXCERPTED: An untitled address presented at the Bethany Pentecostal Mission Room, Pudsey, 5 September 1925, 1-2.

Faith Is an Act

In the beginning was the Word, and the Word was with God, and the Word was God. All things were made by him; and without him was not any thing made that was made.
John 1:1,3

We are saved by faith and kept by faith. Faith is a substance. It is also an evidence. God is. He is! He is a rewarder of them that diligently seek Him. We are living in the inheritance of faith because of the grace of God, saved for eternity by the operation of the Spirit.

All was made by the Word. I am begotten by His Word. Within me there is a substance that has almighty power in it if I dare believe.

Faith Principle #9

Faith goes on to act. It's a reality,

a deposit of God, an almighty flame moving you to act, so that signs and wonders are manifest.

A living faith within the earthen casket. Are you begotten? Is it an act within you? Some need a touch, liberty to the captives. As many as He touched were made perfectly whole. Faith takes you to the place where God reigns, where you are imbibing God's bountiful store. Unbelief is sin.

Pray this closing prayer today:

Jesus, You have created all that is. I desire to act on Your Word and to live by the power of Your Word. Amen.

Excerpted: "Floodtide," Faith Leaflet No. 2, 3-4.

The Author of Our Faith

Looking unto Jesus the author and finisher of our faith; who for the joy that was set before Him endured the cross, despising the shame and is set down at the right hand of the throne of God.

Hebrews 12:2

He is the author of faith. Jesus became the author of faith. God worked this plan through Him by forming the worlds, by making everything that there was by the word of His power. Jesus was the Word; Christ. God so manifested this power in the world, forming the worlds by the word of Jesus.

God's divine principle is that God hath chosen Jesus, ordained Him, clothed Him and made Him greater than all because of the joy given by the love of God.

Because of this exceeding, abundant joy of saving the whole world, He became the author of a living faith.

Faith Principle #10

We are changed by this faith from grace to grace.

We become divine inheritors of God's promises.

Pray this closing prayer today:

Jesus, author of all faith, write the joy of Thy faith onto the pages of my life. Amen.

EXCERPTED: "Faith (Part Two)," message presented at Glad Tidings Tabernacle, 3 August 1922, 5.

Righteousness by Faith

And be found in him, not having mine own righteousness, which is of the law, but that which is through the faith of Christ, the righteousness which is of God by faith.
Philippians 3:9

Oh, if I could, by God's grace, pour into you the difference between our every day righteousness and that attitude of a living faith that dares claim and believe in Him! For I perceive there is something after the righteousness of faith that you can never get by the righteousness of the law.

There is something in imputed knowledge and righteousness of God which is greater than all beside. David speaks about it. Paul often speaks about it. But I want to bring just a touch of it on the lines of faith in Abraham's life.

Abraham believed God, and it was counted

unto him for righteousness. It was an imputed condition. God came forth and said to all the demons in hell and all the men on the earth, "Touch not that man."

Faith Principle #11

If you get to know God's righteousness, if you get to know the faith of righteousness, you can dare to stand and face anything in the world!

You can count on God to bring you through on all lines for "no weapon that is formed against thee shall prosper" (Is. 54:17).

Pray this closing prayer today:

Lord, by faith impute Thy righteousness that I might stand even against the forces of hell. Amen.

EXCERPTED: "That I May Know Him," message presented at Glad Tidings Tabernacle, 20 August 1922, 4-5.

Faith Is the Victory!

*Above all, taking the shield of
faith, wherewith ye shall be able
to quench all the fiery darts
of the wicked.*

Ephesians 6:16

Remember that God our Father intensely desires for us to have all the full manifestation of His power so that we need nothing but His Son. We have perfect redemption. We have all the power of righteousness. We have to understand that we are brought into line with all of God's power, dethroning the power of the enemy.

If you are afflicted in any way, do not for a moment under any circumstances come to the conclusion that the devil has enmity against you. No, he never has. The devil has nothing against you. But the devil is against the living Christ and wants to destroy Him. If you are filled with the living Christ, the devil is anxious to get you out of the way, thereby destroying Christ's power.

Faith Principle #12

Say this, "Now, Lord, look after this property of yours." Then the devil cannot get near.

When does he get near? When you dethrone Christ of the rightful position over you, in you and through you, the devil gains a foothold in you. I preach faith, and I know it carries you through if you dare believe it. You will be strong if you believe it. Faith is the victory — always. Glory to Jesus!

Pray this closing prayer today:

Lord Jesus, by faith I claim Your victory over the devil. Amen.

EXCERPTED: "Ephesians 4:1-16," Bible study no. 9, 19 July 1927, 10.

Faith
Without Charity

*And though I have the gift of
prophecy, and understand all
mysteries, and all knowledge; and
though I have all faith, so that I
could remove mountains, and have
not charity, I am nothing.*
1 Corinthians 13:2

Suppose I had all faith so I could remove mountains; and I had a big farm, but there was some of my farm land that was not very profitable. It was stony, had many rocks upon it and some little mountains on it that were absolutely untillable and no good. But because I have faith without charity, I say, "I will use my faith, and I will move this land. I do not care where it goes so long as my land is clean." So I use my faith to clear my land.

The next day my poor neighbor next door comes and says, "I am in great trouble. All your wasteland and stony, rocky land has been tipped onto mine, and my good land is spoiled."

And I, who have faith without charity, say to him, "You get faith and move it back!" That profits nothing.

Faith Principle #13

If God brings you to a place of faith, let it be that your faith is for the glory of God.

Then when you pray, God will wonderfully answer you. Nothing will hinder your being used for God. Gifts are not only useable, but God is glorified in Jesus when you pray the prayer of faith. Jesus said, "When ye pray believing, the Father shall be glorified in the Son."

Pray this closing prayer today:

Heavenly Father, fill me with Thy love so that I might be used of Thee to glorify Thy name whenever I exercise faith. Amen.

Excerpted: Bible study no. 8, 15 July 1927, 8-9.

Faith Will Be Tested

*Therefore being justified by faith,
we have peace with God through
our Lord Jesus Christ: By whom also
we have access by faith into this
grace wherein we stand, and
rejoice in hope of the glory of God.
And not only so, but we glory in
tribulations also: knowing that
tribulation worketh patience; And
patience, experience.*
Romans 5:1-4

Do you want to have a big story to tell?
Well, here it is. Count it all joy in the midst of
temptations. When the trial is severe, when
you think that no one is tried as much as you,
count it all joy. When you feel that some
strange thing has so happened that you are
altogether in a new order, count it all joy.
When the trial is so hard you cannot sleep,

count it all joy. God has something for you in the trial, something divine, something of a divine nature.

Faith Principle #14

You are in a good place when you do not know what to do.

After Abraham was tried, then he could offer Isaac — not before he was tried. God put Abraham through all kinds of tests. For twenty-five years he was tested. He is called the "father of the faithful" because he would not give up when he was under trials. We have a blessing today because one man dared to believe God without moving away from Him for twenty-five years.

Pray this closing prayer today:

Jesus, when I am under trials, experiencing temptations and facing tests, when I don't know what to do, I shall lean wholly on You. Amen.

EXCERPTED: "Temptation Endured," Bible study no. 12, 22 July 1927, 3.

Ask and Believe

And all things, whatsoever ye
shall ask in prayer, believing,
ye shall receive.
Matthew 21:22

God wants us every day to be in a rising tide. God wants us to come into the place where we will never look back. It is a changing faith and an attitude of the spirit. It is where God rises higher and higher.

Faith Principle #15

God wants us to come into the place where we will never look back. God has no room for the man who looks back, thinks back or acts back.

The Holy Ghost wants to get you ready for

stretching yourself out to Him, believing that He is a rewarder of them that diligently seek Him. You need not use vain repetition. Ask and believe.

People come with their needs. They ask. They go away still with their needs because they do not faithfully wait to receive what God has promised them. If they ask, they will get it. Do more believing and less begging.

Pray this closing prayer today:

Jesus, I come to Thee asking, not begging, to receive all that You have for me. Give me the patience to faithfully wait to receive what You have promised to me. Amen.

EXCERPTED: "Workers Together With God," Bible study no. 15, 28 July 1927, 1.

The Leap of Faith

*Jesus saith unto her [Martha], Said
I not unto thee, that, if thou
wouldest believe, thou shouldest
see the glory of God?*
John 11:40

You have to take a leap today. You have to leap into the promises. You have to believe that God never fails you. You have to believe it is impossible for God to break His Word. He is from everlasting to everlasting.

Forever and ever, not for a day
He keepeth His promise forever;
To all who believe, to all who obey,
He keepeth His promise forever.

There is no variableness with God. There is no shadow of turning. He is the same. He manifests His Divine glory.

To Mary and Martha, Jesus said, "If thou wouldst believe, thou shouldest see the glory of God."

Faith Principle #16

We must understand that there will be testing times, but they are only to make us more like the Master.

He was tempted in all points, like as we, yet without sin. He endured all things. He is our example.

Pray this closing prayer today:

Lord, I would take that leap of faith that I might behold Thy glory. Amen.

EXCERPTED: "Temptation Endured," Bible study no. 12, 22 July 1927, 5.

Faith Laughs at Impossibilities

*Jesus said unto them, Because
of your unbelief: for verily I say
unto you, If ye have faith as a
grain of mustard seed, ye shall say
unto this mountain, Remove hence
to yonder place; and it shall
remove; and nothing shall be
impossible unto you.*
Matthew 17:20

Now my soul longs for you to catch fire!
Four things are emblematic, divinely ascertained or revealed by the Lord — *fire, love, zeal, faith.*

Fire, burning up intensely, making us full of activity on line with God.

Love, where there is nothing but pure, undefiled willingness, yieldedness, knowing no sacrifice.

Zeal, so in the will and the mighty power of God until we press beyond measure into that which pleases God.

Faith Principle #17

Faith, that laughs at impossibilities, and cries, "It shall be done!"

May God make these things immediately real before our eyes and give them to us as emblematic displays of inner fire!

Pray this closing prayer today:

Lord Jesus, set me ablaze with fire, love, zeal and faith. Amen.

EXCERPTED: "This Grace," Bible study no. 26, 19 August 1927, 1.

Daring to Believe the Atonement

*And not only so, but we also joy
in God through our Lord Jesus
Christ, by whom we have now
received the atonement.*
Romans 5:11

Atonement is "at-one-ment." Perfect association is being at one in Christ. Whatever His appointment in the earth, whatever He was, we have been joined up to Him in "one-ment." The atonement is "one-ment," meaning that He has absolutely taken every vestige of human deformity, depravity, lack of comprehension and inactivity of faith and has nailed it to the cross. It's forever on the cross. You died with Him on the cross. If you will only believe you are dead with Him, you are dead indeed to sin and alive to righteousness.

The atonement, the one-ment principle, the working out of this wonderful, regenerative power of God is, "I am complete in His oneness."

There is not a vestige of human weakness in His righteousness. If I dare believe, then I am so in order with God's Son that He makes me perfect, at one with Him, no sin, no blemish, no failure, absolutely a perfect atonement till there isn't a vestige of weakness left.

Dare you believe it? It may not be easy for you, but I want to make it easy. Faith is the substance of things hoped for. Everything the Word of God speaks to you, faith lends its help. Faith stirs you. Faith says, "If you believe, it is now." If you dare believe now, then oneness, purity, power and eternal fact are working through you.

Pray this closing prayer today:

Lord Jesus, I believe that Thy atonement makes me one with Thee. Amen.

EXCERPTED: "This Grace," Bible study no. 26, 19 August 1927, 7.

Trusting an Extravagant God

Bless the Lord, O my soul: and all that is within me, bless his holy name. Bless the Lord, O my soul, and forget not all his benefits: who forgiveth all thine iniquities; who healeth all thy diseases; who redeemeth thy life from destruction; who crowneth thee with lovingkindness and tender mercies; who satisfieth thy mouth with good things; so that thy youth is renewed like the eagle's.

Psalm 103:1-5

As I see it, Scripture is extravagant. When God speaks to me, He says, "Anything you ask." When God is speaking of the world's salvation, He says, "Whosoever believes." So I have an extravagant God with extravagant language to make me an extravagant person — in wisdom.

If you have extravagancies without wisdom, you will know very well it is going to be no profit. You have to learn not to leak out or waste.

Faith Principle #19

You must learn above all things that you have to be out and God must be in you.

The trouble with many people is that they never have gotten out so that He could get in. But if God ever gets in, you will be the first one out, never to come in anymore.

Pray this closing prayer today:

Jesus, by faith I go out that all of You might come in. Amen.

EXCERPTED: "God Bless You!," Bible study no. 4, 8 July 1927, 6.

Have a Real Faith

*Therefore whosoever heareth these
sayings of mine, and doeth them,
I will liken him unto a wise man,
which built his house upon a rock:
And the rain descended, and the
floods came, and the winds blew,
and beat upon that house;
and it fell not: for it was founded
upon a rock.*
Matthew 7:24-25

Are you ready? What for? To believe the Scriptures. That is necessary. The Scripture is our foundation to build upon properly. Christ is the cornerstone. We are all in the building.

Claim your rights in God's order. Do not give way. If you hear any spiritual breathing from anyone, believe that is your order. If you see Christ, believe He was your firstfruit.

Have faith in God. Believe the Scripture is for you. If you want a high tide rising in the power of God, say, "Give me, Lord, that I shall be short of nothing."

Have a real faith. Believe that love covers you. His life flows through you. His quickening Spirit lifts you.

Pray this closing prayer today:

Heavenly Father, I claim the foundation of Thy Word for Thy answer to my every need. Amen.

EXCERPTED: "Workers Together With God," Bible study no. 15, 28 July 1927, 14.

Believing as a Son of God

But as many as received him, to them gave he power to become the sons of God, even to them that believe on his name.

John 1:12

Be as a son of God. A son of God must have power over the powers of the devil. A son of God must behave himself seemingly. A son of God must be temperate in all things. A son of God must have the expression of the Master. He should be filled with tenderness and compassion. He should have a body filled with bowels of mercy. A son of God must excel in every way.

Faith Principle #21

God says about you more than you dare say about yourself.

"Behold, ye are sons of God." So do not be afraid. Take a stand. Come into line. Say, "I will be that."

God spoke and the heavens gave place to His voice. God proclaimed, "This is my beloved son...hear ye him" (Matt. 17:5). Afterwards, Jesus always said, "I am the Son of God."

God comes to you and says, "Behold, you are sons of God!" Oh, that we could have a regiment rising, claiming their rights, standing erect with a holy vision and full of inward power, saying, "I am, by the grace of God, a son of God!"

Pray this closing prayer today:

Lord, by Thy grace I trust in Thee and claim that I am Your son, Your daughter, Your child. Amen.

EXCERPTED: "Sons of God," Bible study no. 7, 14 July 1927, 7.

Unwavering Faith

*If any of you lack wisdom, let him
ask of God, that giveth to all men
liberally, and upbraideth not; and it
shall be given him. But let him ask
in faith, nothing wavering.*

James 1:5-6

I am satisfied that God, who is the builder of divine order, never brings confusion in His order. If you want this divine order in your life, if you want wisdom, you have to come to God believing. I want to impress upon you the fact that if you ask six times for anything, it shows you are an unbelieving person.

Faith Principle #22

*If you really believe, you will ask
God only once, and that is all you
need because He has abundance
for your every need.*

But if you go right in the face of asking once, and ask six times, He knows very well you do not mean what you ask, so you do not get it.

God does not honor unbelief. He honors faith. For example, if you ask God once for healing, you will get it. But if you ask a thousand times a day till you forgot what you were asking, you're not asking in faith. If you would, ask God for your healing now, then begin praising Him. He never breaks His promise. You would go out perfect. "Only believe."

Pray this closing prayer today:

Lord, I set aside confusion and wavering for single-mindedness and faith. I come to You asking once in faith. I stand on Thy Word, not my vain repetitions. Amen.

EXCERPTED: "Temptation Endured," Bible study no. 12, 22 July 1927, 10-11.

Precious Faith

*Simon Peter, a servant and an
apostle of Jesus Christ, to them that
have obtained like precious faith
with us through the righteousness of
God and our Saviour Jesus Christ.*
2 Peter 1:1

Faith in Jesus Christ gives us access to the fullness of God. It was by grace first. You were saved through grace. But now we have another grace, a grace of access; a grace of entering in; a grace of understanding the unfolding of the mystery; a grace which shall bring us into a place of the knowledge of God.

In 2 Peter, we have a very special word which will help us here. In the first verse, there is one special thought we should dwell on: "like precious faith." We have received like precious faith from all those who have passed through faith by grace.

All that the Father has, all that Jesus has, all the Holy Ghost has, we have access into.

We have the right and an open door into all that God has for us. There is nothing that can keep us out. Jesus Christ is the Alpha and Omega for us, that we may know grace, favor and mercy to lift us into and take us through.

"Grace and peace be multiplied unto you through the knowledge of God, and of Jesus our Lord" (2 Pet. 1:2). You want grace multiplied? You want peace multiplied? You have it here if you dare to believe. We have access to the Father by faith through His grace.

Pray this closing prayer today:

Thank you, Father, for the grace through Jesus Christ that You have bestowed on my life. Amen.

Excerpted: "This Grace," Bible study no. 26, 19 August 1927, 3.

Rest in Faith

*For we which have believed do
enter into rest.*

Hebrews 4:3

When the divine has the full control, then all earthly cares and anxieties pass away. If we live in the Spirit, we are over all human nature. If we reach the climax God's Son said we had to come into, we shall always be in the place of peace.

Jesus said, "If ye abide in me, and my words abide in you, ye shall ask what ye will, and it shall be done unto you" (John 15:7). Jesus was the manifestation of power to dethrone every evil thing. He always dealt with the flesh. It was necessary for Him to say to Peter, "Get thee behind me, Satan: for thou savourest not the things that be of God, but the things that be of men" (Mark 8:33). Everything that interferes with your plan of putting to death the old man is surely the old man comforting you, so that you will not act to crucify the flesh.

Faith Principle #24

There is a rest of faith if we have entered into it. This rest of faith ceases from our own works, ceases from our struggling, ceases from making our own plans.

It is a rest in faith, a place where you can smile in the face of any eruption. No matter what comes, you will be in the place of real rest. Hear the Savior say, "Come unto me, all ye that labour and are heaven laden, and I will give you rest. Take my yoke upon you, and learn of me; for I am meek and lowly in heart: and ye shall find rest unto your souls" (Matt. 11:28-29).

Pray this closing prayer today:

By faith, Lord, I enter into Thy rest in which there is perfect peace. Amen.

Excerpted: "2 Corinthians 3," Bible study no. 16, 29 July 1927, 2.

One
Faith

*There is one body, and one Spirit,
even as ye are called in one hope of
your calling; One Lord, one faith,
one baptism, One God and Father
of all, who is above all, and
through all, and in you all.*
Ephesians 4:4-5

Just in the proportion that you have the Spirit unfolding to you — "One Lord, one faith, one baptism" — you have the Holy Ghost so incarnated in you, bringing into you a revelation of the Word. Nothing else can do it, for the Spirit gave the Word through Jesus. Jesus spoke by the Spirit that was in Him, being the Word. The Spirit brought out all the Word of Life. Then we must have the Spirit.

If you take up John's gospel, you will find that when He came, it wasn't to speak about Himself but to bring forth all that the Father willed. "For all things that I have heard of my Father I have made known unto you" (John 15:15).

Faith Principle #25

Just as we have the measure of the Spirit, there will be no measure of unbelief.

We shall have faith. The Church will rise to the highest position when there is no schism in the body on the lines of unbelief. When we all with one heart and one faith believe the Word as it is spoken, then signs, wonders and various kinds of miracles will be manifested. There will be one accord, in "One Lord, one faith, one baptism." Hallelujah!

Pray this closing prayer today:

Lord God, by Thy Spirit we shall confess One Lord, Jesus, and be of one faith in Him. Amen.

EXCERPTED: "Our Calling (Part Two)," message presented at Glad Tidings Tabernacle, 22 August 1922, 5.

holy Faith

*But ye, beloved, building up
yourselves on your most holy faith,
praying in the Holy Ghost, Keep
yourselves in the love of God,
looking for the mercy of our Lord
Jesus Christ unto eternal life.*
Jude 1:20

I saw one day a great big magnet let down amongst iron, and it picked up loads of iron and carried them away. That is a natural order, but ours is a spiritual order of a holy magnet. That which is in thee is holy. That which is in thee is pure. When the Lord of righteousness shall appear, who is our life, then that which is holy, which is His nature, which is His life, shall go, and we shall be forever with the Lord.

You have not gone yet — but you are sure to go. Seeing we are here, comforting one another, building up one another in the most holy faith, we would say, "No, Lord, let it please thee that we remain. But please, Father, let us be more holy. Let us be more pure. Please, Father, let this life of Thy Son eat up all mortality till there is nothing left but that which is to be changed, in a moment, in the twinkling of an eye."

Do not let one thought, one act, one thing in any way interfere with more rapture.

Faith Principle #26

Ask God that every moment shall be a moment of purifying, a moment of rapture seeking, a moment in your body of a new order of the Spirit.

Let God take you into the fullness of redemption in a wonderful way. Covet to be more holy. Covet to be more separate. Covet God. Covet holy faith.

Pray this closing prayer today:

Please, Father, build in me a holy faith that I might be totally set apart unto Thee. Amen.

EXCERPTED: "This Grace," Bible study no. 26, 19 August 1927, 13.

Faith That Trusts

*And such trust have we through
Christ to God-ward: Not that we
are sufficient of ourselves to think
any thing as of ourselves; but our
sufficiency is of God.*
2 Corinthians 3:4-5

We want to get to a place where we are beyond trusting ourselves. Beloved, there is so much failure in self assurances. It is not bad to have good things on the lines of satisfaction, but we must never have anything on the human plane that we rest upon.

Faith Principle #27

There is only one sure place to rest upon, and our trust is in God.

In Thy name we go. In Thee we trust. And God brings us off in victory. When we have no confidence in ourselves to trust in our God, He has promised to be with us at all times, to make the path straight and to make a way. Then we understand how it is that David could say, "Thy gentleness hath made me great" (2 Sam. 22:36).

Ah, thou Lover of souls! We have no confidence in the flesh. Our confidence can only stand and rely on the One who is able to come in at the midnight hour as easily as at noon day and make the night and the day alike to the man who rests completely in the will of God, knowing that "all things work together for good to them that love God," and trust Him. And such trust have we in Him. The Lord has helped me to have no confidence in myself but to trust wholly in Him, bless His name!

Pray this closing prayer today:

In Thee, Oh Lord, do I place all my trust. I will not trust in myself or human flesh, only in Thee. Amen.

EXCERPTED: "Ye Are Our Epistle (Part One)," message presented at Glad Tidings Tabernacle, 23 August 1922, 3.

Faith
Lets Go

*Let us lay aside every weight, and
the sin which doth so easily beset
us, and let us run with patience the
race that is set before us, Looking
unto Jesus the author and finisher
of our faith.*

Hebrews 12:1-2

How may I get nearer to God? How may I be in the place of helplessness in my own place and dependent on God? I see a tide rising. "Blessed are the poor in spirit: for theirs is the kingdom of heaven" (Matt. 5:3).

God is making us very poor but we are rich in it, because our hands are stretched out towards God in this holy day of His visitation to our hearts.

Believe that He is in you. Believe that He is almighty. Believe that He is all fullness.

Smith Wigglesworth ❈ 59

Faith Principle #28

Let yourself go till He is on the throne. Let everything submit itself to the throne and the King.

Yield yourself unto Him so that He is perfectly over everything. Let God have His perfect way through you.

If you will let go, God will take hold and keep you up. Oh, to seek only the will of God, to be only in the purpose of God, to seek only that God shall be glorified, not I! What a word we get over and over in our hearts, "Not I, but Christ."

Pray this closing prayer today:

Jesus, I trust You. I let go that You might be all in all. Amen.

EXCERPTED: "The Riches of His Glory," Bible study no. 14, 27 July 1927, 12.

Faith and Grace

Therefore, it is of faith, that it might be by grace; to the end the promise might be sure to all the seed; not to that only which is of the law, but to that also which is of the faith of Abraham; who is the father of us all.

Romans 4:16

I want you to see that you can be healed if you will hear the Word. Some need healing. Some need salvation. Other desire sanctification or the baptism of the Holy Spirit. God's Word says, "by faith, that it may be by grace." Grace is omnipotent, active, benevolent and merciful. Grace is true, perfect and an inheritance from God that the soul can believe.

Grace is of God. It is by faith. You open the door by faith, and God comes in with all you want.

Now, healing comes by faith and not by feeling. Some even want salvation by feeling and say, "Oh, if I could feel I was saved." It will never come that way. Faith acts on a fact. A fact brings joy. So you hear the Scriptures, which make you wise unto salvation, opening your understanding, so that if you hear the truth and believe, you will receive what you want. By faith you open and shut the door. By grace, God comes in — saving, healing and meeting your needs.

Pray this closing prayer today:

Father, I thank You for Thy grace. By faith I open the door of my life to receive all that is in Thy grace — thy salvation, healing and blessings in Jesus Christ. Amen.

EXCERPTED: "Faith," message presented at Good News Hall, Melbourne, Australia, 1922, 3.

Living Faith

*That your faith should not stand in
the wisdom of men, but in the
power of God.*
1 Corinthians 2:5

Faith has the power of access. Living faith is unfeigned faith; faith that never wavers. Faith comes from the Author of faith.

Faith Principle #30

This faith is like Jesus, holy in act, daring to believe, resting assured and seeing the mighty power of God made manifest through this living faith.

By a living faith in God, the crooked are made straight, the lame leap with joy and the blind are made free.

*Lord Jesus, birth into me Thy living faith.
Amen.*

EXCERPTED: "This Grace," Bible study no. 26, 19 August 1927, 4.

The Wigglesworth Series

The following thirty-day devotionals
are also available.

Smith Wigglesworth on Prayer

Smith Wigglesworth never read any other
book than the Bible. He viewed prayer
as an act of faith that claimed the truth
of God's Word as a sure foundation for
victory in all of life's trials. Discover
timeless insights into God's Word and
prayer as you use this devotional.

Smith Wigglesworth on Healing

Smith Wigglesworth believed that every
believer could be baptized in the Holy
Spirit and that God could perform miracles
today as He did in the early church. Grasp
these truths as you use this devotional to
inspire and encourage your own faith.

Available at your local Christian
bookstore or from:

Creation House
600 Rinehart Road
Lake Mary, FL 32746
1-800-283-8494